Trail of Thought

Trail of Thought

Deep Poems To Ponder On

TAHIR FRANCIS

Library of Congress Control Number:		2022910076
ISBN:	Hardcover	978-1-6698-2705-4
	Softcover	978-1-6698-2704-7
	eBook	978-1-6698-2703-0

Print information available on the last page.

Rev. date: 05/26/2022

To order additional copies of this book, contact:
Xlibris
844-714-8691
www.Xlibris.com
Orders@Xlibris.com
842720

Acknowledgement

The most difficulty I had in writing this book was finding inspirations and unrooting my emotions then transitioning it in the words that the audience may feel some relatedness to the topics of each poem. Even though I may not be the most emotionally verbal person, I truly feel expressive when listening to R&B music which was one of my main muse in writing most of the poems.

My family: you have always been there for me providing support, love and an abundance of encouragement to achieve in whatever I see fit.

Glory goes to God for aiding me in my creativity and guidance in finishing this book, I've fought through procrastination and writer's block to get this completed.

Mentors, special friends who I have learned so much and made a positive influence in my life. Too many to mention one by one but you know who you are. I appreciate the impact you all have had in my life.

My respected readers: you are the driving force that helped me, as this book was only an idea but you've made it tangible. I look forward to your participation, feedback and involvement.

Contents

Chapter 3: Sticks and stones may break my bones, but your words hurt

Chapter 4: Fool me once, shame on you

CHAPTER 1

He loves me, He loves me not

Oil + Water

A foreseeable reaction happens when we try to fuse
I try to voice my side but you stick to your views
Like Oil and Water, we are bad chemistry
We could not get along, everyday felt like misery
Let's go our separate ways, find someone that fuels your ego
As I search for a partner that will douse me up with attention

Jungle Love

Passion grew on me like flowers in the spring,
Anticipating your tulips to be planted on my face,
Your smile radiates my spirit making me long for you more.
Like a sea, your touches keep me calm like the sound of the shores,
If this is jungle love I'll use your body as a map and eagerly explore.

Physical

To me you look forward in giving you comfort
Overwhelmed by your love but I can't get enough
Understanding from the start so I know this isn't lust
Come to me and feel safe when I wrap you in my arms
How only just your presence supplies me tranquility.

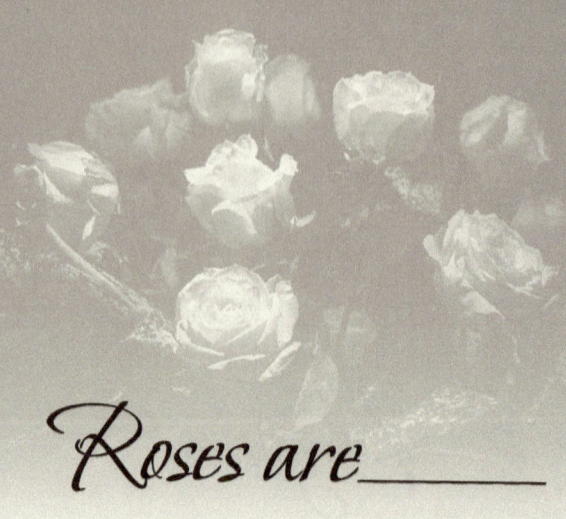

$\mathcal{R}$oses are_____

Blue means secret admirer for the way I keep you intrigue
Yellow stands for friendship and cheer
White ties with the suggestion of marriage and spirituality
Pink could represent my outgoing elegance and grace
Red is the best way to confess your love
Orange aligns with enthusiasm and passion I have around you
Colorful thoughts in your mind, the decision is only on you to choose
and buy
As I wait and see which rose am I

Plain Sight

I have always been there, you just never wanted to look
3 years and 7 months is the time it took
For you to finally notice I was here
Opaque must be your vision because my actions made it clear
That I want you
When your eyes light up to show you're excited
When your lips pout out because you're sad
I feel bliss being in your company
I just know in my gut that you are the one for me
Happy to see that your trick is over and the magic can start
You finally see me; I just hope your willing to share your heart

Traits

Reckless, Insecure, Pessimistic
These are the side effects of not taking my daily dose of you
Courageous, Perceptive, Rhapsodic
These are the traits you've built within me
My self-awareness finally kicked in, as I realize you are now just
memory I have to cherish
For your soul stays with me but your life has perished.

Hopeless Romantic

An abundance of love fuels my happiness
I feel this was destined to be, I chose you and you chose me
Swept off my feet by your passionate kisses
I am already fantasizing of being your Mrs.
My friends try to keep me level headed and be wary of you
Are we rushing this too fast, will this be something I may rue?
Be honest and give me your sensible judgement so I won't be the
romantic fool

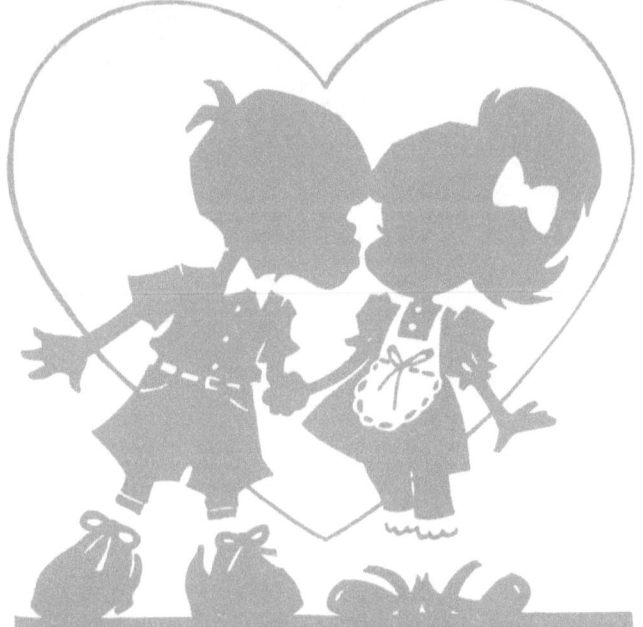

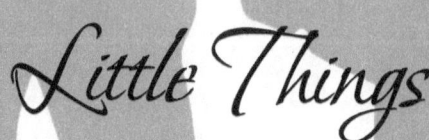

Little Things

The way you caress my back to soothe me to sleep
Document our special moments to relish on
Always keeping yourself approachable making it easy to speak my
mind
You keep me on my toes with surprises of gifts and date ideas
I love handing you flowers just for you to plant your kisses on me
Even an atheist can see that you are heaven sent
Money doesn't matter, being around you is time well spent
You don't ask for much but anything you need I'll tend
It's the little things that makes me grateful to have you as a partner
and a friend

Memories

I knew in my heart that you held back on more
Closing me off, you left my feelings tore
Happiness and memories fade into dust.
I gave you love, attention and trust.
But that commitment was broken when you searched for lust.
I knew it wasn't real love when we started to rust.

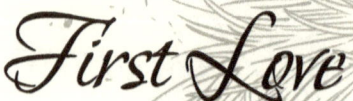 First Love

Building the courage to approach you,
Words scatter in my mind to form a speech
Sweaty palms surface, as I mumble your name
I look away to ease my nerve-racking brain,
Is this the feeling of love or am I just a coward?

ABC'S

Please B close to me when time feels lost,
I need your attention 'N' love but at what cost?
C, your presence gives me peace and keeps me reassured.
But when you're distant, I don't know anymore.
Like R U the one I want or someone I need?
Y can't you love me at my own speed?

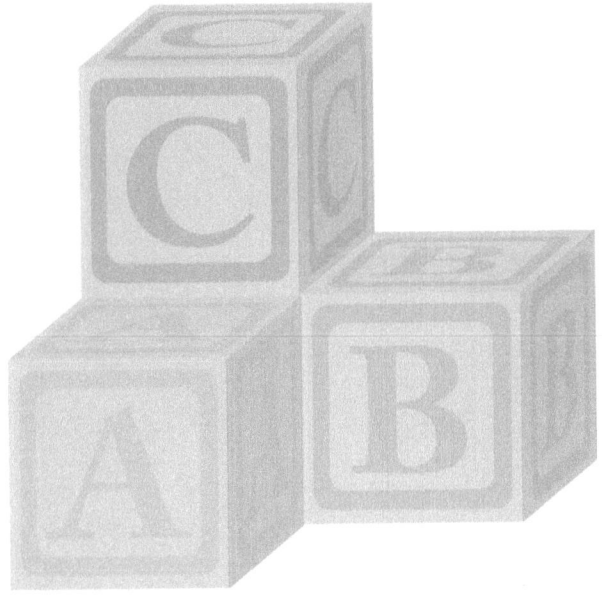

Only One

Four you to make me feel special, I need clarity and sincerity
Stop entangling me in this threesome with you and your demented
thoughts
Two take this on a next level, boundaries have to be placed
I should never be questioned as an option
Just second to none
Figure out your intentions and make me the only one

Apologies

I am sorry I was not the person you wanted me to be,
You realized my imperfections and started to see,
My true nature was rabid, myself expression was jagged,
A pitiful boy lost in his own mind, whom you gave your heart and care with divine.

Looks < Personality

Infatuated by your looks
I neglected your personality
Lost in thought, of what we could be
Finally, it took me a while to face reality
How shallow could I have been, to put your appearance before what's inside?
Your sweet smiles cloaked your tasteless sense of humor
I found myself trying to spice up conversations, only to receive bland responses
Ultimately, I've come to terms on what the truth is
I need someone who has values and charisma to the core
Good looks aren't enough, I need more

IOU

Borrowing a lot of your time and affection
I have some catching up to do
You deserve the world and more
I owe you loyalty, attention and adoration
I owe you generosity, peace, and care
I owe you gratitude, gifts of my appreciation and acts of service to
your needs
I am indebted to you
How do you want to be paid?
In lumpsum which I hope isn't too much to take in all at once
Or installments where I can recur my admiration until you're satisfied

Action vs Words

I am loud as can be when I show you my intentions
Supplying you with gifts and hugs to ease any tensions
Why speak about mistakes, when I could display what I've learned
Because trust doesn't feel the same when it's handed out and not earned

Hearing you voice your concerns,
Why wait for me to react, when I can quickly please you with words
Soft spoken, I can simply give more when I speak only the truth
Because you know my affirmations are needed to keep you soothe

CHAPTER 2

The grass is greener on the other side

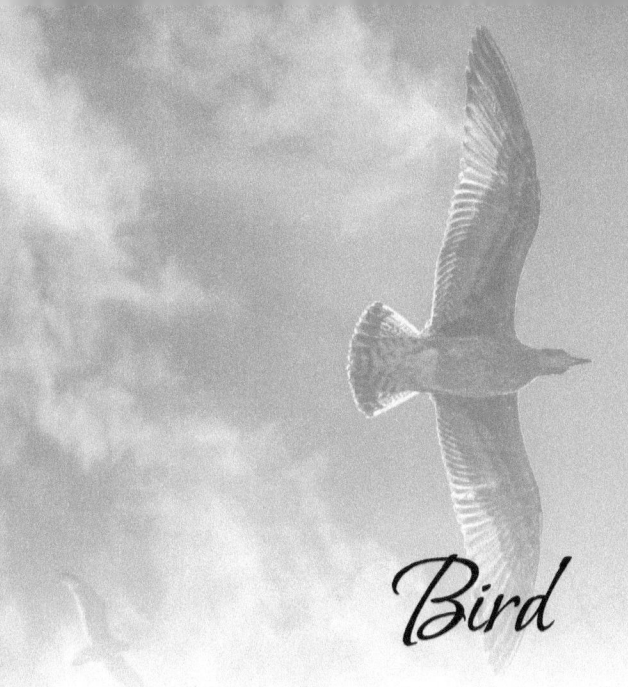

Bird

Be free in your mind and in the open,
Inspire others to be creative and live in the moment.
Realize your potential and aim for the skies,
Soar above greatness like a bird that flies.

Lean On

When you've lost all strength in your body, reach out and ask for help
Not all problems can be dealt just by yourself
Let me help you carry your burdens
That's what friends are for
To make sure your wounds are seal and recovered, not to leave them bore
I will stand tall for you, when your hardship is too much to bare
Just lean on me and know that I will be there

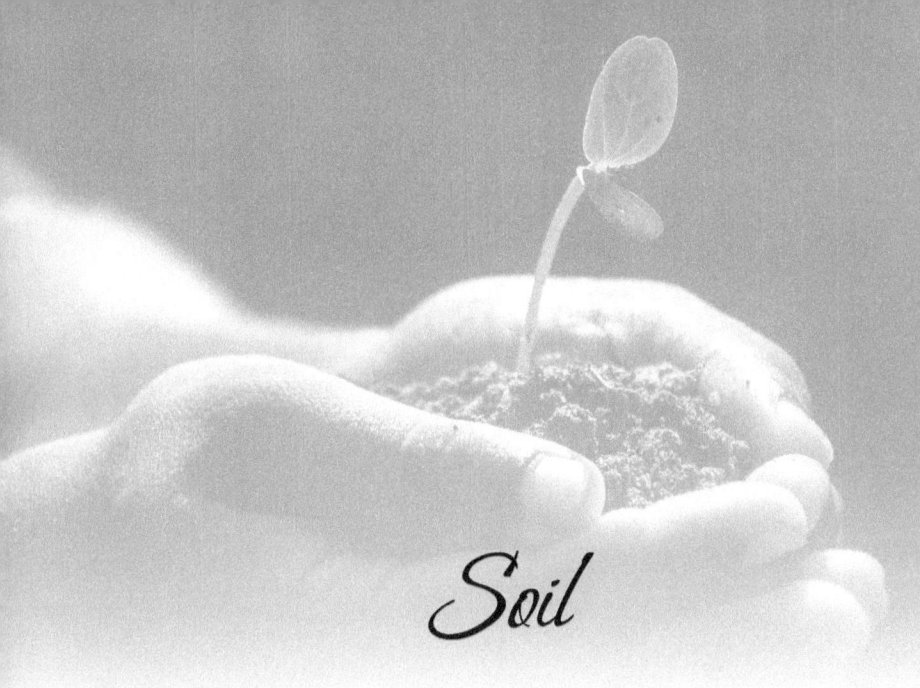

Soil

Here sets the foundation for my roots
As I begin to grow
My environment delivers an impact of how I may live
Will I receive good sun light and water to help me blossom?
Or will the bigger trees take all the nourishments for themselves?
Born in dirt, I was already expected to amount to nothing
But with perseverance and luck there's a chance I can make me it out
A little glisten of hope opens up when I start sprout
Growing where society despises you of being spoil
But the truth of their envy comes from being planted in
malnourished soil

Food

I love being your favourite source of pleasure,
Our bond gets stronger as the years go by.
Been there for you in bad break ups and celebratory moments.
Whether happy or sad I'm still a mood,
Some know me as pizza, Ice-cream or fries but I prefer food.

Phone

Carried in your arms,
I am always by your side,
Like a new born baby you show me off with pride.
Knowing that this relationship would be temporary from the start,
I'll cherish you in my data frame until an upgrade do us apart.

Sun

I illuminate this land with hope and green trees,
Educate people with high degrees.
A lot of things admire me like chicks, bananas and even cheese.
My biggest fans of all are the bumblebees.
I was here before life begun,
I am the father of all stars but they call me Sun.

Shadow

I tend to fall behind and rarely step in front
Easy to bare, I don't burden your body having to carry me around
At least you acknowledge me in your bright moments rather than dark
Everyone seems to have me but do they want me?
Each morning I lay at your feet in your chateau
Waiting for your steps to follow as your devoted shadow

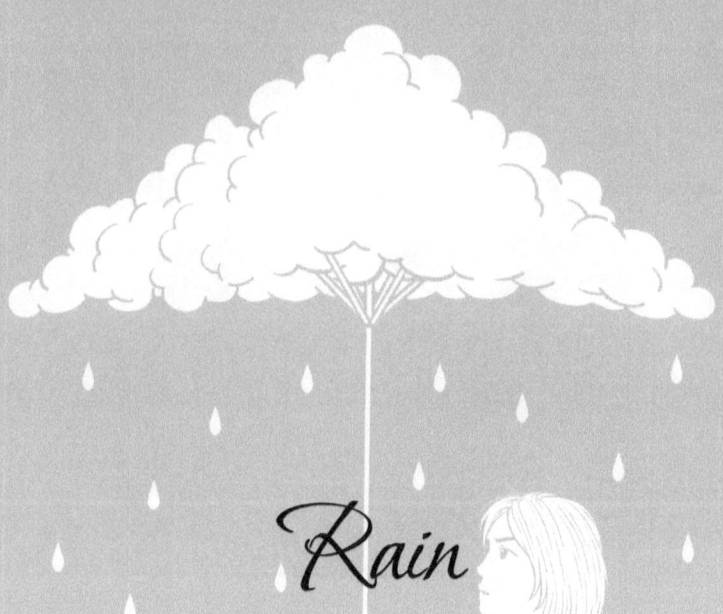

Rain

Does it fuel your sadness or brings peace?
It nurtures life all around us but yet we run for shelter than marvel at its work
A soothing calmness it brings at night ushering us to sleep
Glooming aura, we describe it as when it appears at day
Just like a coin it has two appearances to whomever sees it
But in the end, it still functions the same just rain

She's Someone

She wears her heart on her sleeve, emotionally strong and physically capable
Her presence is priceless, I never question what she brings to the table.
Women are made out of affirmation and self-love, with God's Grace they're able
They overcame everything that was meant as a set back
Took a challenge head first and was never kept off track
You were mold out this earth just from love, ribs and clay
So, stand tall and be proud of the woman you are today.

Birth

Through the force of gravity, we push and pull,
Through the force of life, we push and scream.
Coached on your first view of life by a nursing team.
I've been an abundance of joy since birth
Now I roam this land to find my worth

Mom

You've given me structure when there was no foundation.
Showed me the importance of faith, family and education.
Provided an abundance of hugs, kisses and compassion.
Guided me on the right path when I am tempted by distraction.
Your qualities are infinite I have a list of things to say,
You were built to be a mother in every way.

Dream

Stirred by our subconscious mind
It boils over into our daily thoughts
Seasoned with ideas of how to prep for it and make this tangible
I hunger to feel fulfilled with a purpose on how to be happy
Think it, believe it, say it and declare it
Simple but powerful actions that help you achieve your dreams

Meaning of Life

It's a gift that can't be wrapped
But you can toss it away or make something of it
Cherish every moment whether joyful or sorrowful
It doesn't matter what you amount to, just the lives you've impact
Sons and daughters carry on our legacy
Providing and teaching them to be a better version of me

Empty

Like a bottomless well I hold hope that I may be filled someday to
quench my thirst.
Life has thrown me under the rug to hide me from the worse.
The truth I lock away from myself when I know the answer is in mind,
That only God, can replenish this empty soul of mine.
But experience has shown that it is sometimes fake or envy
So, I hold onto hope and pray for rain
That this empty well may be filled once again.

Drive

Stuck in park I don't know if I can complete my journey
Do I have enough fuel to get me to my destination?
Or should I standby and hope someone can take me there instead?
Trying to avoid these contradicting thoughts
But I have a habit of going in reverse when I'm close
Parked car conversations have my mind in profundity
I question myself of what's holding me back?
How do I find my drive to get back on track?

CHAPTER 3

Sticks and stones may break my bones, but your words hurt

Accountability

You choose the easy way out and ghost me
Instead of showing me respect and taking accountability
I thought what we had was real but you just lead me on
Now I am stuck making adjustments since you've been gone
Conflicted in my mind if I was the one that pushed you away
Or were you just not honest enough to say you wouldn't stay

Scar

The damaged you've left visually remains, but internally I've healed
Your astounding imitation of love fooled me to be real
Buried inside, the pain and heartbreak I had to conceal
Left me witless and out of touch on how to feel
I won't let you get the best of me! Life is a classroom full of lessons
So, I've embraced my mistakes and started learning how to love my scar
Next time I will be cautious and leave my feelings only ajar

Insecurities

Blessed is the meekness
Built up a wall to lock in my insecurities
For society sees them as weakness
Why parade something around if you won't laud
When I know some sinister souls only want me to open up to jeer at me
Cold stares, and silent judgement gives me the sense of feeling flawed
So, I stay patient, eventually my walls will crack
Sowing affirmations on myself, I wait for my confidence to grow back

Questions

How did I not see this from the start, when your persona turned harsh, cold and dark?
You would turn something from positive to negative leading an argument to spark.
I had to get out, knowing that a toxic relationship is not where I belong
Now I am left all alone, pondering in my thoughts of what went wrong?

Self-Sabotage

I'm a ticking time bomb when it comes to liking someone new,
My rambled thoughts got me thinking it's too good to be true.
Are your intentions real or is it a facade?
One moment things are great, the next it's odd.
Why do I put a guard up and block my own happiness?
Why do I distance myself from the people who want to get close?
Maybe contentment for me will only stay a mirage,
Funny how they say, "Keep your enemies close," maybe that's why I
self-sabotage.

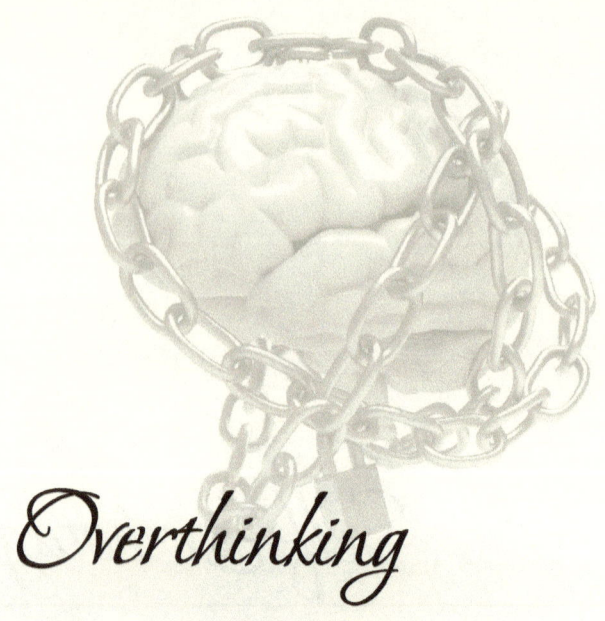

Overthinking

Will you love me forever or just in the moment?
I question your actions when I feel uncertain,
Reassurance is what you give with your words, but your actions play a
different tune.
Your sweet talk and gentle touch lead us to courtship,
But every time I speak my mind you want to jump ship.
Kindness and affection are the only thing I plead.
Overthinking is my curse; I need to be freed.

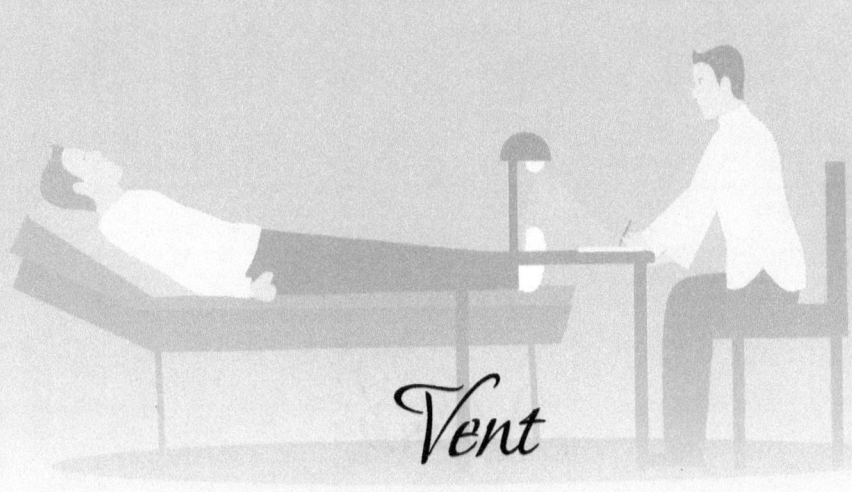

Vent

If I suppress my feelings, I will eventually lash out on the innocent
Caged in emotions need to be released
It's just I don't want to be a burden on others with my problem
Or worse, I express my thoughts and it's thrown back at me
Transitioned from a jovial person to apathetic, now in the stages of
agony
It's sad to feel the only one I can trust is written in contract
Because no one takes the time to reach out and make contact
On Thursday afternoons my family wonders where I flee
It's to vent to my best friend that sits across from me

Numb

Warm to the touch, cold in the heart,
That last bad break up was when it had start.
Feelings and emotions have been erased,
Use to fall fast in love but I've slowed my pace.
You played with my mind recklessly like a guitar or a drum,
I don't know how to grieve, you've made me numb.

Damaged

She'd rather open her legs before her feelings.
Her heart has been emptied from too much bleeding,
Numb to the pain, she'd preferred being physically hurt than
emotionally scarred up,
Been attacked all her life that's why she keeps her guard up.
Why judge a book by its cover if you won't flip a page,
Her true feelings are locked in her mind, like a bird in a cage.
You can buy her time but not her love,
The only man she claims is the One up above.

Blindsided

Hidden from my peripheral vison
I seem to be unaware of your existence
What a predator you are
As you lie in wait for me to feel most safe
Then attack with daggering critiques
"I would love you more if you had a better physique."
"I like how you are, but can your personality be tweaked?"
"Stop crying all the time, it makes you look weak."
I could never be good enough
Stunned by your words, I feel blindsided

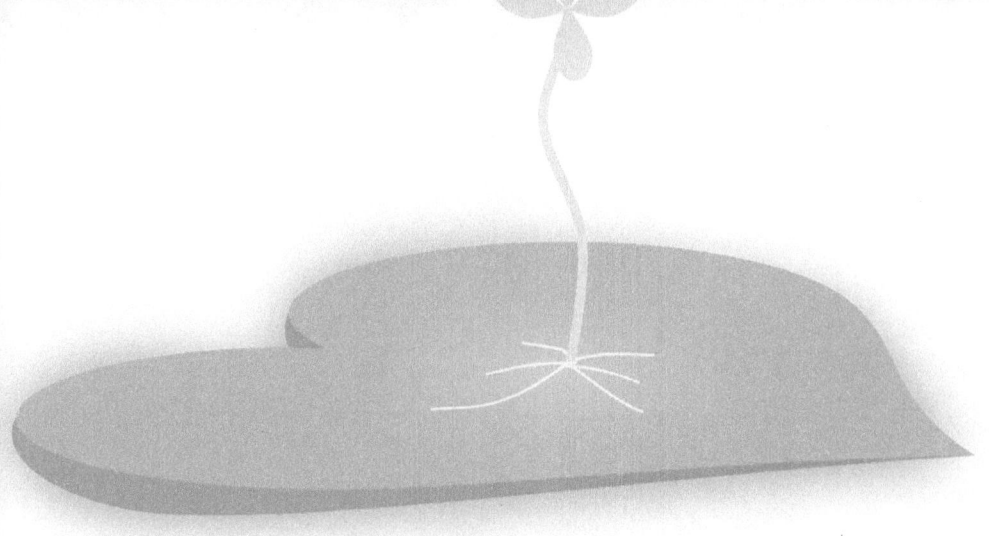

Seeds

They say love is in the air,
I guess I forgot how to breathe.
I've satisfied my wants but not found someone I need.
Been fed up with giving my heart,
Hearing lies and getting deceived,
But love takes time to grow like a plant, too bad I've already emptied
my bag of seeds.

It's not you, it's me

Succumb to my inner thoughts, my lips finally freed what I've sealed within
An angel you are, shouldn't have to bare my sin
Actions done in the shadows, that I have dreaded to be seen in light
My childish persona overtook, things done that look out of spite
Guilty paints my face, when I stand before you waiting on judgement
Emptying out my conscious, I just want you to see
Who is in more desperate need of growth on goodwill, openness and integrity?
It's not you, it's me.

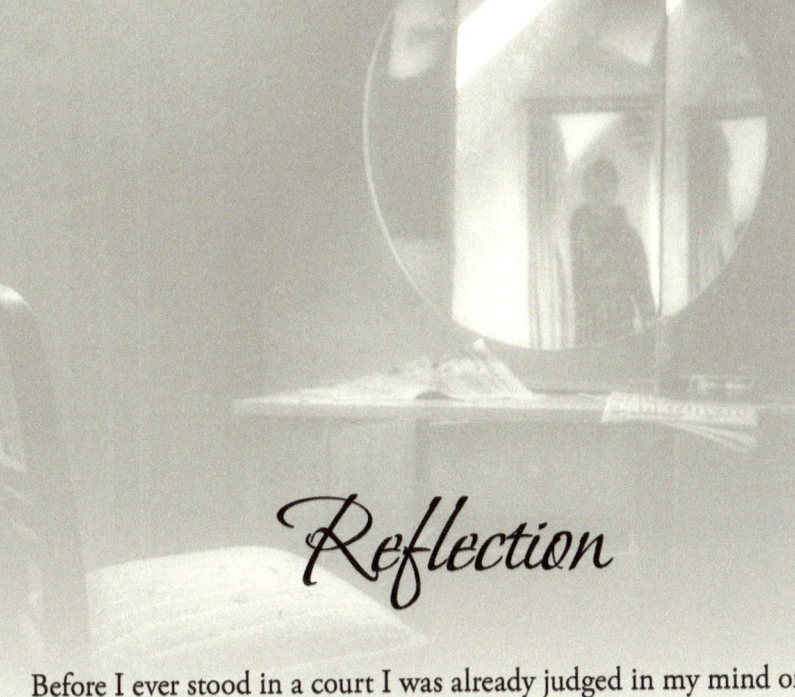

Reflection

Before I ever stood in a court I was already judged in my mind or a mirror
"Why did you do this to yourself?" I question my other half
Consistency and passion are what I lack to find my path
The pressure of life to do well and be successful
But this adulting stage of life has been so stressful
Reflection hurts me more than you think, because what I do to myself affects others
Comparison of my peers has kept my ambitions smothered
This secret I share only to myself or in therapy
But I hold onto optimism that there could be a better me

CHAPTER 4

Fool me once, shame on you

Wasted Tears

Faithful years,
Turned into wasted tears,
This pain in my heart, I cannot bare,
We've fell out of love this was my greatest fear.
It is time to face the truth that out my life you're gone,
I have to gather my strength just to move on.
Leaving you behind I take a final glance,
Broken inside knowing that I'd give you another chance.

Baggage

No one reaches out to help me carry this load
They take a glance and assume a heavy burden it may be
Why not take a moment and ask what's inside?
An interest in what I have, to me alone is a peculiar surprise.
You would be shocked to know how easy it can be managed
Because I've only packed a light baggage

Stranger

I knew you inside out
Inseparable, you couldn't rip us apart
Once thought of how our lives would turn out 30- 40 years from now
I guess I got too ahead of myself when we couldn't make it pass an
anniversary
A familiar face you were until I hit CTRL + ATL + DLT
Now your existence seems to be forgotten
As we continue our lives as strangers

Figures

Memories begin to form when I think of adding you back in my life,
You circle my thoughts at least once a day,
Let me shape up my actions 2 be the partner you need and not want,
But I can't stop lying to fill my own greed,
Figures, why you left me.

This way

This way

Lost

Was on the right path 'til I took a wrong turn,
I tried to make my way back but the bridges were burned.
I was too at ease thinking I knew my way,
But an unfamiliar path is where I had stray.
Looking for an exit to escape my mind and this place,
But a dead-end every turn, I make, is what I face.
I am lost.

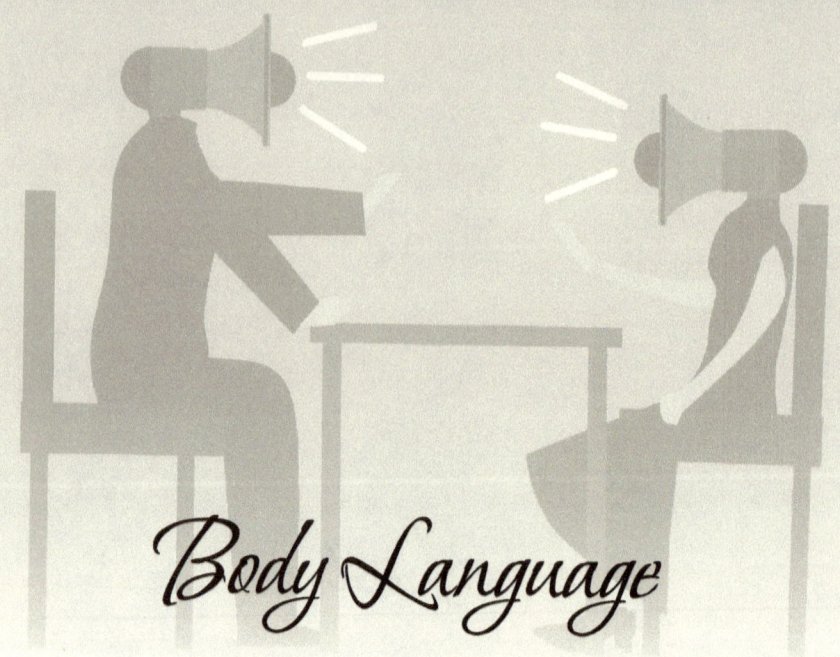

Body Language

My body gesture speaks for itself, when I feel annoyed or nervous
Frustration masks my face when I don't get my way
Arms open up to show that you're ready to me embraced
But a cold shoulder I give to keep your endearment at bay
It seems you don't understand me anymore.
I try to translate how I feel but communication has been a developing problem
Should we seek assistants from a translator to break this barrier,
Or sacrifice the time to learn each other's language?

Self-worth

Why give you my all when I receive just a fraction
Your presence alone doesn't give me satisfaction
I did some growing up and I can clearly picture a life without you
Instead of fessing up about your lies you insist of being framed
I am to be treasured not a prize to claimed

Irony

Life gives you lemons but you give me heart aches
One minute we're in the love, the next argument you want a break
I feel stupid for prioritizing your feelings before my own,
Thinking you'd be the one to understand me and be my home
But in the end, you sold me lies and left me with remorse
Knowing you were wrong but you always play the victim of course
Now I see why manipulation begins with man

Fade

My feelings circles back
I try to regain my emotions to please you with affection
But I can't shake the fact that I don't show the same attention

My feelings revisit from time to time
I try to regain my emotions to have control
But a part of me still feels missing, to be completely whole

My feelings come and go
I try to regain my emotions but the process has been slow
The truth I've tucked aside because I was afraid
That feelings for you have started to fade

Promise

You've brought my existence to life with your binding words
My value holds strong for trades of hope and trust
But be careful how you portray me
Because I can easily be broken without touch
On attack my name is brought up in things that should be done
On defense my life seems to be paired up with God
You keep me close to your heart in moments of belief
But once I've been completed, my creator feels relief

Investment

Nervousness takes over, it's my first-time learning about you,
I listened to your goals and plans in queue.
Give it time and have patience is what I'm advised,
Should I take a risk and roll the dice?
Will I reap the investment that I sowed in this crop,
Or will it turn out to be another bad stock?

Space

Don't take this the wrong way

You have always been special to me

We've been through thick and thin even uncertainty

it's just, i feel stifled some times i'm with you

Can't blame you for being clueless, let's just take this in a positive way
to try something new

I plead my love for you again

Before you judge my case

Emotionally attached but physically

Need some space

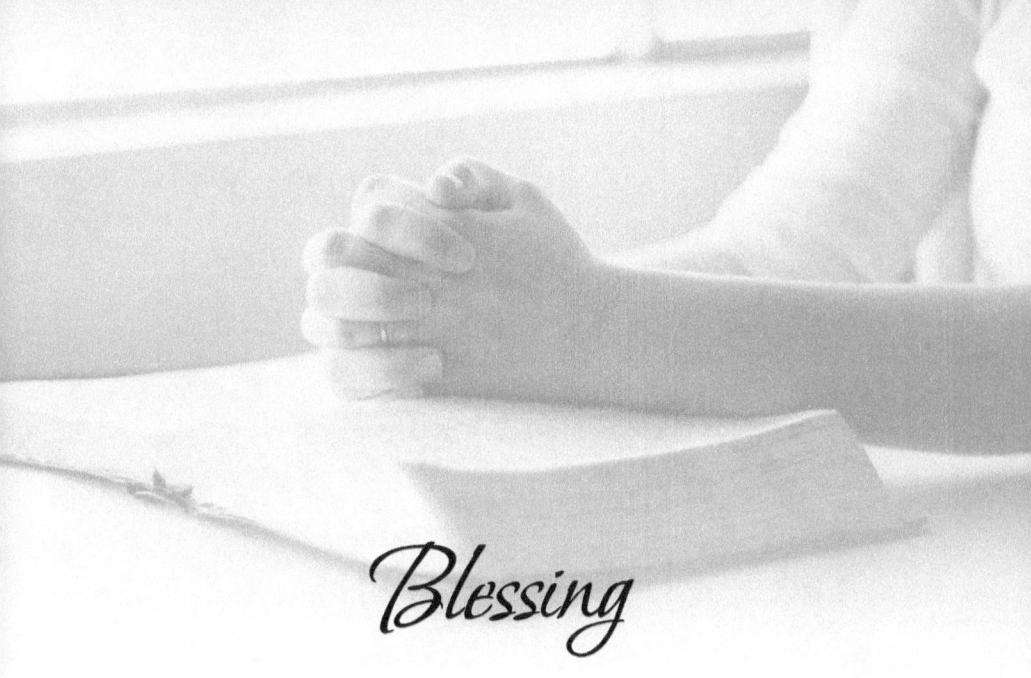

Blessing

I don't need your pity, I'm already miserable enough
I wallow in my mistakes,
holding onto my ego, I find someone to blame for my misfortunes
Led astray by bad choices of friends, partners and even parental
guidance
It's their fault I'm like this! I should've known better than trust
naively,
Am I forever cursed or will my troubles pass with time?
I want to be better and learn from these life lessons
In hopelessness I turn to religion
As I pray and ask for a blessing

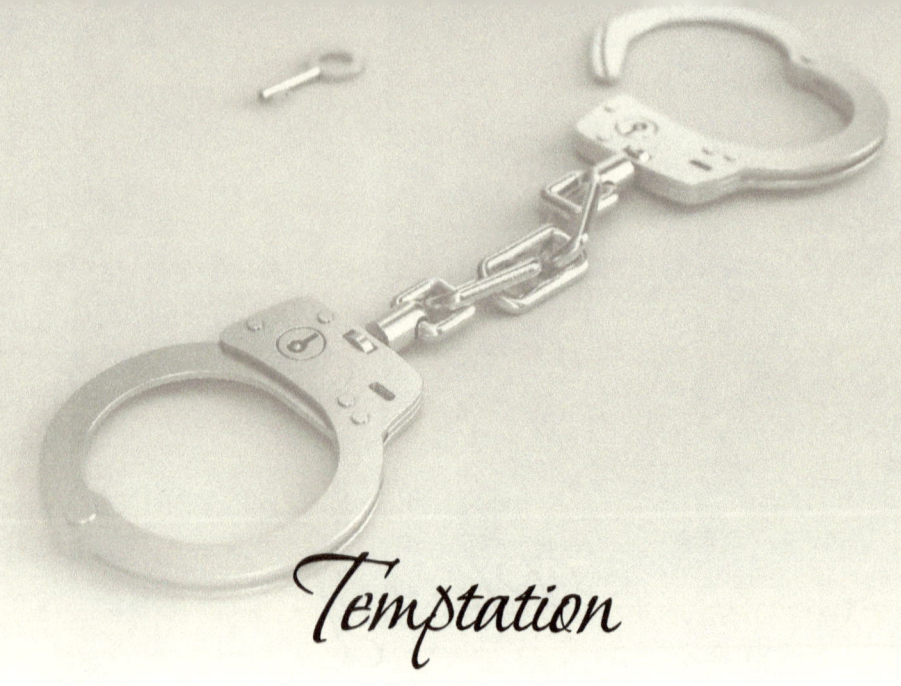

Temptation

If it's the desire to do something wrong
Then why don't I feel any guilt about my actions?
A slight smile and harmless flirting are all I do
But my mind seems to day dream when I am around you
Is it the need to feel wanted that piques my interest?
Or that I'm using this as void to not fix something that I already have
The remedy of what to do is being aware, reflect and act.
Since what I thought was a solid foundation has revealed some cracks
Do I tear down and rebuild this project or would starting something new be easier?
Tempted away by my thoughts, I need to find how to have some clarity
Because I can't be giving my love and time away like some charity

Foggy Night

Navigating through this sightless path, I trust my mind to lead
the way,
With each small step it feels like a leap of faith.
My vision is dimmed so I rely on my senses,
But sticking by your side I was told that's senseless.
Lost in this world I can't tell who my friend is,
Having no one in my corner, so I always feel defenseless
Stuck in this fog I don't know where the end is.
I need some guidance.

2 minds, 1 body

Great minds think alike but your thoughts defer from mine
My lower half controls my actions, while my upper sways my feelings
Torn between on what to do and how to perceive
Stressed out, my body has grown peeve
Can't we just agree on one thing? And not be so stubborn to have our own way
Whether right or wrong it's my body that is stuck with the sin to be weigh

Vacancy

There is a vacancy for love so I'm screening the best candidate to
move in,
I have evicted all my toxic traits and made room for a companion
Someone who is seeking to build a foundation and settle down
Not rent from place to place and barely be around
My doors are open and the exit signs are clear
But who I keep in my space I have to stay aware?
So, I will remain patient by playing my cards smart
Even though I want a partner finding a good roommate is a start

Hide 'n' Seek

Your presence is here but emotions are hidden, for the fear of being
disappointed again,
Tucked away to never to be seen
But I avidly seek to find what you have buried and who to embrace
You've concealed all your flaws making it harder to trace
Come out where ever you are! So that I may find you
Tired of these games, let me show the world what I view
Beauty, and playful with a heart full of kindness
It makes sense why it was you who hide, because it would be hard to
seek with blindness

www.ingramcontent.com/pod-product-compliance
Lightning Source LLC
Chambersburg PA
CBHW030940240526
45463CB00015B/835